Earth Buddy ™ is a trademark of Seiger Marketing, whose co-owners Anton Rabie and Ronnen Harary were two unemployed Generation Xers when they sat around the kitchen table considering the possiblities of a creature that Harary's grandmother had just brought back from Israel. With the addition of superior seed from Oregon and fine untreated sawdust, Rabie and Harary created a product that has sold 1,000,000 units in North America.

Debora Pearson is a freelance writer and editor. Her work as Editor of *OWL* magazine, helped it win numerous awards. She is the author of *Alphabake: A Cookbook and Cookie Cutter Set*.

Jane Kurisu was born and educated in Toronto, Ontario. A graduate of Sheridan College, her work has appeared in advertising and various magazines and children's publications, including *Alphabake: A Cookbook and Cookie Cutter Set*.

A Somerville House Book
SCHOLASTIC INC.

READY, SET, GROW!

WITH THE EARTH BUDDIES

By Debora Pearson
Illustrated by Jane Kurisu

SCHOLASTIC INC.
New York   Toronto   London   Auckland   Sydney

If you purchased this book without a cover, you should be aware that this book is stolen property. It was reported as "unsold and destroyed" to the publisher, and neither the author nor the publisher has received any payment for this "stripped book."

No part of this publication may be reproduced in whole or in part, or stored in a retrieval system, or transmitted in any form or by any means, electronic, mechanical, photocopying, recording, or otherwise, without written permission of the publisher. For information regarding permission, write to Scholastic Inc., 555 Broadway, New York, NY 10012.

ISBN 0-590-62986-7

Copyright © 1995 by Somerville House Books Limited.
All rights reserved. Published by Scholastic Inc. by arrangement with Somerville House Books Limited.

12 11 10 9 8 7 6 5 4 3 2 1   5 6 7 8 9/9 0/0

Printed in Canada
First Scholastic Printing, November 1995

Many thanks to Lorraine Johnson, Master Composter, Jane Snyder of the Recycling Council of Ontario, and gardening expert Mark Cullen, each of whom provided valuable assistance with the composting activity. Thanks also to Carol Anne Campbell of the Canadian Museum of Nature for reviewing the manuscript. And finally, a special word of appreciation to Barbara Hehner whose skillful editing and encouraging words helped this book flourish and grow.

AN IMPORTANT NOTE FOR KIDS AND GROWNUPS

When activities need something to be cut with a knife or scissors, everyone has to be extra careful. If you see this 🖐 sign on an activity in this book, it means that a grownup should help out.

TABLE OF CONTENTS

- **4**   Meet the Earth Buddies
- **6**   It Starts with a Seed
- **8**   Get Growing!
- **10**   Put on a Seed Show
- **14**   Be a Seed Spotter
- **16**   Tops and Bottoms
- **18**   Trick Some Stems
- **20**   Try Bean Push-Ups
- **22**   Who Wants Water?
- **24**   Make Water Run Up
- **26**   Soak It with Paper
- **30**   Make "Acid Rain"
- **32**   Fun in the Sun
- **34**   Head for the Shade!
- **36**   Growing, Growing...Gone
- **38**   Getting to the Root of the Matter
- **40**   Make Some Compost
- **44**   You Can Do It!
- **47**   Words That Will Grow on You

MEET THE EARTH BUDDIES

It's time to get to know the Earth Buddies! Take them out of the box and gently squeeze them. Earth Buddies are filled with sawdust and covered with a nylon "skin." Now look at the tops of the Earth Buddies. Do you see lots of little dark flecks? Each fleck is a grass seed that can grow into a plant. And as the seeds sprout and the blades of grass grow, they will also become your Earth Buddies' "hair"!

Your Earth Buddies need your help to start growing. This book will show you what to do. It will also show you lots of other ways to have fun with your Earth Buddies (and other simple materials) as you uncover the secrets of seeds and plants. You can make an Earth Buddy's hair grow sideways, watch beans do push-ups, and mix up a batch of "acid rain." While you do these activities, you'll be learning lots of things to help you take care of other seeds and plants, and keep them green and healthy. Plants are everywhere — so get growing!

IT STARTS WITH A SEED

What's so special about a seed? It's the part of a plant that can sprout into a new plant. Some seeds are tiny, like the grass seeds in your Earth Buddy. Others, like the seeds of a double coconut tree, can be enormous. Just one of these seeds weighs as much as a five-year-old

child! But big or small, heavy or light, all seeds are the same inside. Each one holds a tiny baby plant, called an *embryo,* that grows into a larger plant. Right now, the grass seeds in your Earth Buddies don't look as if they are about to change into grass plants. But when you give them three things — water, warmth, and light — something amazing happens: the seeds wake up and start to grow.

GET GROWING!

What happens if the seeds in an Earth Buddy get warmth and light but no water? Will they still wake up and grow? Here's one way to find out.

WHAT YOU NEED:

2 Earth Buddies   **2 dishes**   water

WHAT YOU DO:

1. Put one of the Earth Buddies in a bowl of water, and hold it there until it sinks to the bottom on its own. This takes about 2 to 3 minutes.

2. Place the Earth Buddy in a dish. The top of its head, where its "hair" will grow, should be facing up.

3. Put the dish in a warm, sunny place. There should always be a little water in the bottom of the Earth Buddy's dish. Keep your Earth Buddy moist but do not overwater it.

4. Place the second Earth

Buddy in the other dish so the top of its head is facing up.
5. Put it in a warm, sunny place, but don't water it.
6. Wait 7 to 10 days.

WHAT HAPPENS:

The seeds in the first Earth Buddy have all three things they need to grow — water, warmth, and light — so they *germinate,* which means they start to sprout. Seven to 10 days later, the baby plants have grown big enough to see as tiny shoots. But what about the second Earth Buddy? Even though its seeds got lots of warmth and light, they couldn't grow because they had no water.

After you have done this activity, give the second Earth Buddy water, warmth, and light so its seeds will start to sprout, too. Just take care of it the same way you took care of the other Earth Buddy.

PUT ON A SEED SHOW

Most seeds, including the ones in your Earth Buddies, are buried and out of sight when they first sprout. But you can watch some other seeds as they start to grow — and put on your own seed show at the same time!

WHAT YOU NEED:

dried kidney beans and lima beans (these are the seeds)

big glass jar with a wide mouth

dark-colored construction paper

paper towels

scissors

water

magnifying glass

WHAT YOU DO:

1. Soak the beans in some water for 3 hours.

2. Cut the construction paper so it's as tall as the jar.
3. Roll it up in a tube and put it in the jar.

4. Stuff the paper towels in the center of the jar so that the construction paper presses against the glass.
5. Put the bean seeds in the jar between the construction paper and the glass.
6. Wet the paper towels.
7. Put the jar in a warm place with light, but out of direct sunlight. Keep the paper towels and construction paper moist all the time.

8. To see what a baby plant looks like inside a seed, wait one day, then remove a lima bean from the jar.
9. Gently peel off its covering.
10. Find the edge where the halves of the bean are joined together. Use your fingernails to open up the halves.
11. Check your seed against the picture.
12. If you have a magnifying glass, use it to take a closer look.

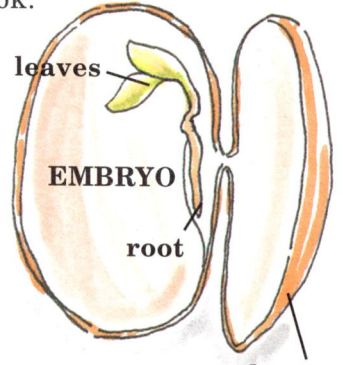

Construction paper and seeds

Root emerges

Young plants come next

WHAT HAPPENS:

Each seed soaks up water like a sponge and swells. The hard covering of the seed splits because it's too small to hold the swollen seed. Inside, the baby plant fills up with the water, making it easier to see when you look inside the seed. A seed's roots sprout first. Then its stem pokes out and little green leaves appear. Your seeds are growing into seedlings!

BE A SEED SPOTTER

Every day, you eat lots of different kinds of seeds or foods made from seeds. Check out the list below for some of the most common ones. Then see how many you can spot in your kitchen.

Popcorn
Each popcorn kernel is a corn seed. When you heat it, the seed's insides expand, burst out, and become a tasty snack!

Peanut Butter
Peanut butter is a paste made from roasted, ground peanut seeds. These seeds ripen underground in papery shells.

Mustard
Mustard is named after the powdered seeds that are in it. These tiny seeds come from the mustard plant.

Bread
Bread is made from flour. Wheat flour is made from the ground-up seeds of the wheat plant. Many kids eat it with another seed treat — peanut butter!

Cocoa
Cocoa powder is added to warm milk to make a delicious chocolate drink. It's made from the roasted, ground-up seeds of the cacao tree.

Rice
Rice grains are the seeds of a kind of grass plant that grows in soggy places. This plant is a cousin of the grass plants that are growing in your Earth Buddies!

Peas
Peas come fresh, frozen, or dried and are the seeds of the pea plant. They grow in rows inside narrow pods.

Granola
This breakfast cereal is usually filled with seeds, including oat seeds, peanut seeds, sunflower seeds, and sesame seeds.

TOPS AND BOTTOMS

Watch some grass in an Earth Buddy for several minutes. Do you see anything happening? You might think the plant is just taking it easy. But from the top of its stem to the bottom of its roots, your plant (like other plants) is hard at work. The stem holds the plant upright. It

also acts like an elevator and sends food made by the leaves down to the rest of the plant. Down at the bottom, the roots are busy, too. First they suck up minerals and water from the ground. Then they send this food up the plant to the stem and leaves in another "elevator." Roots also anchor the plant in the ground and keep it from blowing away. The winter rye plant, a cousin of your grass plants, has extra-long roots for gripping the ground. A single plant's roots can be over 300 miles (483 km) long!

TRICK SOME STEMS

Do stems always grow up? What happens if you move some plants so that their stems aren't pointing up? Have a little stem fun and find out!

WHAT YOU NEED:

Earth Buddy with "hair" at least as long as your index finger

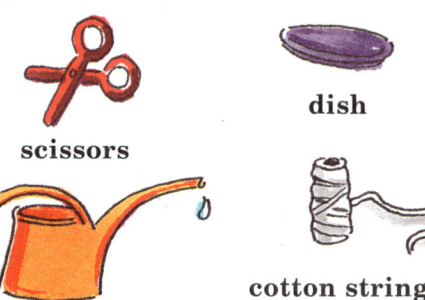

scissors

dish

cotton string

water

WHAT YOU DO:

1. Cut a piece of string as long as your arm.
2. Turn your Earth Buddy upside down, and find the knot in the center of its underside.
3. Tie one end of the string just under the knot, next to the Earth Buddy's "skin." Be sure to tie the string very tightly so that it doesn't slip off.
4. Take the other end of

the string and hang the
Earth Buddy upside down
in a warm, sunny place.
Put the dish under it.

5. Water the Earth Buddy
every day by pouring some
water on it.

6. Keep your Earth Buddy
upside down for 2 weeks
and watch its "hair."

WHAT HAPPENS:

Plant stems respond to sunlight and grow up towards it. When you change the direction the stems face, they bend and turn until they are facing the sun again. This gives your Earth Buddy some wild-looking hair! The roots also turn, although you can't see them doing it. They are responding to an invisible force called *gravity* that pulls things towards the Earth.

TRY BEAN PUSH-UPS

The tops of the Earth Buddy sprouts are strong enough to grow through the nylon "skin" covering them. Even seeds are tough enough to push up things with their tiny stems and roots. You can make your own seed weightlifters and watch them working out!

WHAT YOU NEED:

small glass jar or drinking glass

dried beans (lima or kidney beans work well)

plastic plate

water

WHAT YOU DO:

1. Fill the container with beans.
2. Add water right to the top.
3. Cover the container with the plate.
4. Let the beans sit for 3 hours.
5. Now look at the beans again.

WHAT HAPPENS:

When a seed soaks up water, the stem and roots inside become firm and strong. This extra strength helps them break out of the seed and start to grow. A seed planted in the dirt is strong enough to force away the soil around it as it sprouts. Your bean seeds are mighty enough to knock off the plate that covers them!

WHO WANTS WATER?

What runs straight up a plant without falling down, turns hard seed coverings soft, and makes soft, limp leaves stiff again? Water — and a plant can't live without it. A plant doesn't have any bones to hold its stem straight up to the

sun. Instead, it counts on water to fill the stem and make it stiff. As the plant grows, it also uses water to make food for itself and carry food to other parts of the plant. This drink is so important to a plant that it even has a way to suck water straight up — the way you slurp up a milkshake with a straw. Think about that when you water your Earth Buddies!

MAKE WATER RUN UP

How do plants make water run up without falling back down to the ground? Soak up the answer here!

WHAT YOU NEED:

water

jar or drinking glass

red or blue food coloring

small kitchen knife

celery stalk (stem) with leaves on it

WHAT YOU DO:

1. Put four fingers together and see how wide they are. Pour that much water into your jar or glass.

2. Add lots of food coloring to the water to make it

dark red or blue.

✋ 3. Ask your grownup helper to cut off the end of the celery stalk.
4. Put the cut end in the colored water.
5. Wait 24 hours.

WHAT HAPPENS:

The celery sucks up the colored water through tiny straw-like tubes. The tubes run the length of the plant. When the water rises all the way through the tubes and reaches the top, the leaves turn the same color as the water — red or blue. To see the tubes, take the celery out of the water and ask your helper to cut off the end again. Now look at the cut side. The tiny colored dots are tubes that you have sliced through. Plants have so much sucking power in their tubes that they can pull water straight up into the air — even tall trees get enough water for their leaves this way!

SOAK IT WITH PAPER

How can you water an Earth Buddy when you're not around? Here's a trick you can use if you're away for a day or two.

WHAT YOU NEED:

sprouting Earth Buddy

dish

cotton string

scissors

1 sheet of paper towel

drinking glass

water

WHAT YOU DO:

1. Cut 4 pieces of string, each 6 inches (15 cm) long.

2. Put the paper towel on a table with the long side towards you. Starting at this side, roll the sheet into a loose tube. It should be about as thick as two of your fingers put together.

3. Take one piece of string, wrap it around the top of the tube and tie it loosely. Tie the second piece of string about a third of the way down. Tie another piece two-thirds of the way down, and the last piece of string near the bottom of the tube. Clip off the ends of the strings.

4. Fill the glass with water, almost to the top.

5. Make sure that the top of the water is higher than the Earth Buddy's dish. If it's not, stack books or newspapers under the glass.

6. Put one end of the paper towel tube into the water.

7. Put the other end of the paper towel tube in the Earth Buddy's dish. After an hour or two, check to see how fast the dish is filling with water. If the water is filling it too quickly, lower the glass. If the dish isn't getting enough water, raise the height of the glass a bit more.

WHAT HAPPENS:

The dry section of the paper tube attracts the water and pulls it out of the glass and along the paper towel. When the water reaches the other end, it drips out into the dish and your Earth Buddy soaks it up.

MAKE "ACID RAIN"

Can plants use any kind of water to grow? What happens if you give them a different kind of water? Plunge in and find out more here!

WHAT YOU NEED:

2 sprouting Earth Buddies

dishes

water

vinegar

tablespoon

measuring cup

WHAT YOU DO:

1. Put each Earth Buddy in a dish and place in a sunny, warm place.

2. Mix a batch of "acid rain" by stirring 2 tablespoons (25 mL) of vinegar into 1 cup (250 mL) of water.

3. Give one Earth Buddy

"regular" water from the tap.

4. Give the other Earth Buddy "acid rain." Make sure that there is always some "acid rain" in the dish. When you need more, just mix up another batch.

5. Check your Earth Buddies each day for several days.

WHAT HAPPENS:

The Earth Buddy watered with tap water keeps growing, but the Earth Buddy that receives the vinegar and water starts to die. The batch of water you have mixed is similar to the acid rain that falls in some places in the world. Pollution from cars and factories mixes with water in the air to make acid rain. Like vinegar and water, acid rain is strong enough to kill plants when it falls on them. To stay alive and healthy, plants need clean water. Can you help the Earth Buddy grow again by giving it the clean water it needs?

FUN IN THE SUN

To stay alive and healthy, a plant performs an amazing feat. It uses sunlight, along with water and air, to make its own food. (Other living creatures either eat plants, or eat animals that eat plants. A plant is the only living thing that can turn sunshine into a snack.) To make food, a

plant sets up a food factory in each of its leaves. Its roots suck water from the soil and help send it up to the leaves. At the same time, the leaves take in a gas from the air called *carbon dioxide* and sunlight. A chemical in the leaves that makes them green, called *chlorophyll,* helps the sunlight change everything into food. This process is called *photosynthesis* — and it's one of the best plant tricks around!

HEAD FOR THE SHADE

You wear a hat while you're outside on a sunny day to protect your head from the sun. What happens to an Earth Buddy if it wears a "hat" while it's in the sun?

WHAT YOU NEED:

**Earth Buddy
(one that that hasn't sprouted)**

2 dishes

straight pin

tin foil

water

WHAT YOU DO:

1. Put one of the Earth Buddies in a bowl of water, and hold it there until it sinks to the bottom. This takes about 2 to 3 minutes.

2. Place the Earth Buddy in a dish, with the grass seeds on top.

3. Cut out a circle the size of a quarter from the tin foil.

4. Place the tin foil "hat" on top of the Earth Buddy.

5. Ask your adult helper to stick the pin through the middle of the "hat" so it stays in place.

6. Put the Earth Buddy in a warm, sunny place. Make sure that there is a little water in the dish at all times.

7. Wait 2 weeks, then remove the "hat."

WHAT HAPPENS:

The "hat" blocks out most of the sun and keeps it from shining directly on the seeds. However, there is still enough sunlight around the rim of the "hat" for the seeds there to start sprouting. To reach the sun, they grow sideways under the rim, then up towards the sun. These sprouts are strong enough to push up the edge of the tin foil as they grow. When you remove the "hat," you can see a bare spot on the Earth Buddy's head with a rim of flattened grass around it.

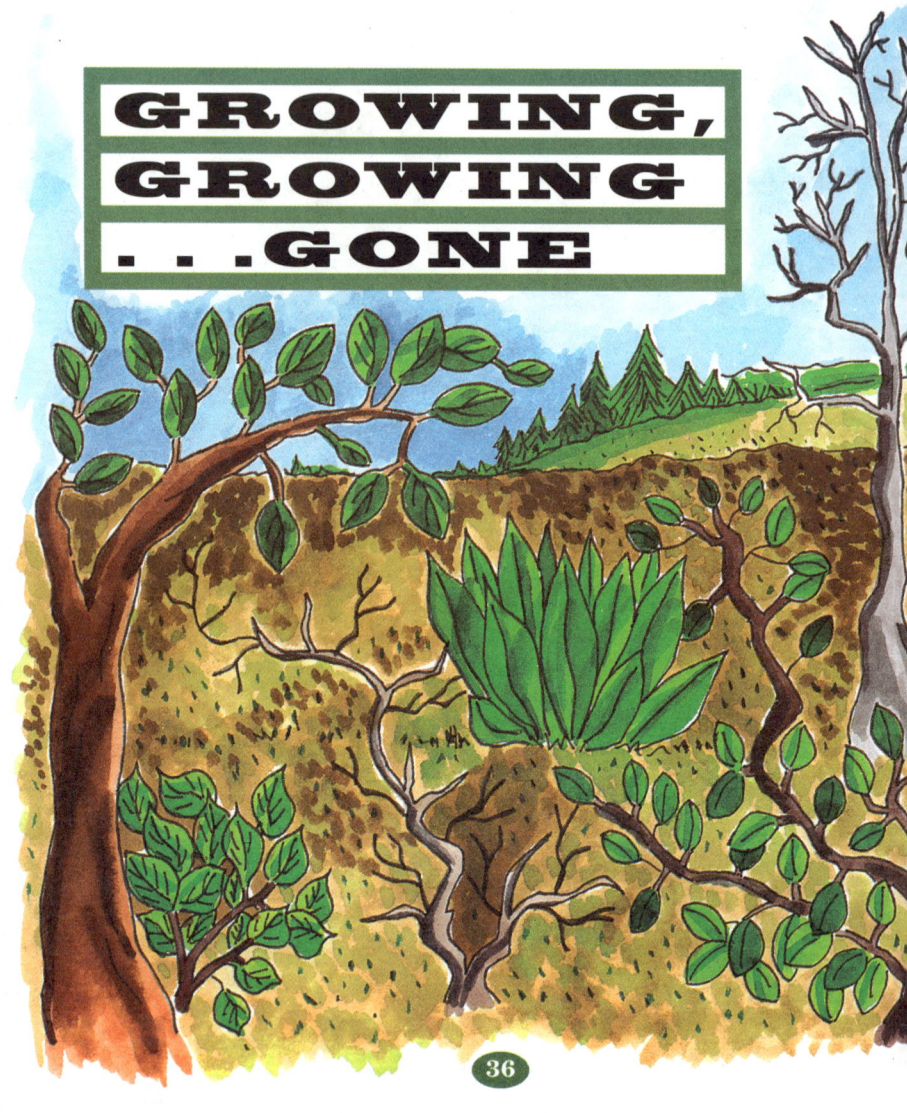

Some plants can live for a long time. A kind of tree in California, called the bristlecone pine, can live to be over 4000 years old! But most plants, including grass, don't live that long. Earth Buddies can live up to two months if they have water, light, warmth, and air. (Of course, if you stop watering your Earth Buddies or give them too much "acid rain," the plants will die sooner than this!)

But don't worry, good things can happen when plants die. They rot and add nutrients to the soil they're in. Soil is like food for plants. Your grass plants aren't growing in soil, but when they die you can help them become "soil food" to help other plants grow.

GETTING TO THE ROOT OF THE MATTER

Want to get the inside story on your Earth Buddy? After it has finished growing, you can open it up and take a look. Don't forget to take out the plants and sawdust and add them to some compost when you are done!

WHAT YOU NEED:

Earth Buddy with dead grass

garbage bag

small kitchen knife

magnifying glass

WHAT YOU DO:

1. Lay the garbage bag on a table.

2. Put the Earth Buddy on the bag.

3. Ask your grownup helper to cut a slit in the

back of the Earth Buddy.
4. Use your hands to break open the Earth Buddy so you can look inside.
5. If you have a magnifying glass, use it to take a closer look.

WHAT HAPPENS:

When you break open the Earth Buddy, most of the sawdust inside it falls apart. Nothing holds the sawdust together once the nylon "skin" is cut. But the sawdust next to the grass and just under the skin doesn't fall apart. It's held together in little clumps by a thin tangled mass of tiny grass roots. These roots still have the empty seeds attached to them. Can you see them? When grass grows in ordinary soil, its roots grab the top of the dirt and keep it from blowing or washing away. Grass is so good at doing this that people plant it in places where they want to protect the soil and hold it in place.

MAKE SOME COMPOST

Compost is a mixture of plant matter that breaks down, or decomposes, and turns into "soil food" that you can give to other plants. Grass clippings from Earth Buddy "haircuts" make great compost ingredients and so does the sawdust from an old Earth Buddy.

WHAT YOU NEED:

restaurant-size pickle jar or any large glass container

dead leaves and sawdust from an old Earth Buddy you have opened up (see page 38)

garden soil

small kitchen knife

spoon

scraps of fruit and vegetables

water

3 long sticks or branches, each as thick as your thumb

fresh grass clippings from your Earth Buddies

WHAT YOU DO:

1. Ask a grownup to help you cut up the fruit and vegetable scraps, grass clippings, and leaves into pieces the size of a lima bean. Make sure there isn't any meat or fat mixed in with the food scraps — they will spoil your compost.

2. Using the spoon, add a layer of leaves or sawdust to the bottom of the jar. Then add the following layers in this order: soil, fruit and vegetable scraps, leaves and sawdust, grass, and soil. Repeat the layers until the container is full.

3. Poke each stick down into the jar as far as it will go. One end should reach the bottom and the other should poke out of the top. Do not put the lid on the jar.

4. Every two days, move the sticks around to add some air to the compost. Do this for about six to seven weeks. Add a little water *only* if the compost gets very dry. (You may not have to do this at all.) After you add water, the compost should be as moist as a sponge with all the water squeezed out. Be careful not to add too much water to the compost or it will stop working and start to smell.

WHAT HAPPENS:

Tiny creatures in the soil feed on the fruit, vegetables, and other plant pieces. As they do, they help the plant pieces decompose and change into dark, rich, earthy food for your plants. Cutting the compost ingredients

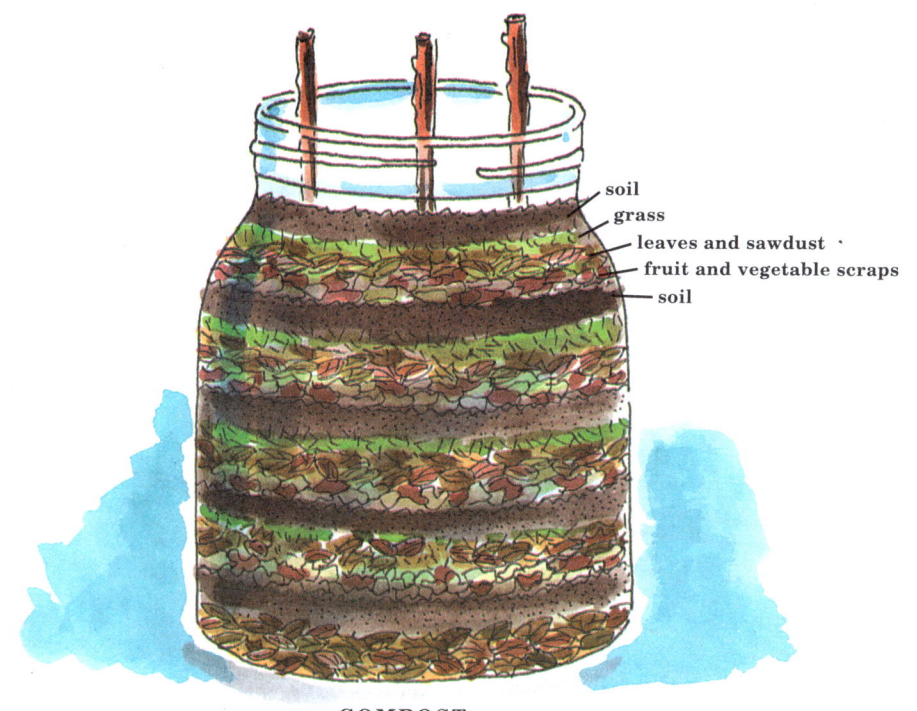

COMPOST

into smaller pieces lets them break down faster. So does adding grass and sawdust from your Earth Buddies. Grass clippings contain a chemical called *nitrogen*. The sawdust (and dried leaves) contain *carbon*, another chemical. Both of these chemicals help the ingredients in the jar break down and turn into compost.

YOU CAN DO IT!

Find out how to make your own Earth Buddy. You can give one to someone you know and show them how to sprout the seeds inside.

WHAT YOU NEED:

1 pair of old nylon pantyhose

scissors

drinking glass with a wide mouth

1½ cups (375 mL) untreated, softwood sawdust from a lumberyard*

2 tablespoons (25 mL) grass seeds: rye grass seed work best

measuring spoon

plastic fishing line

non-toxic fabric paint

*It is very important that the sawdust be untreated, and from softwood. Treated lumber and some hardwoods are poisonous to grass seeds.

WHAT YOU DO:

✋ **1.** Cut off one leg of the pantyhose so that you have a piece as long as your forearm, with the toe at one end.

✋ **2.** Cut a piece of fishing line the same length. Set it aside.

3. Drop the toe end of the nylon piece into the drinking glass. Stretch the cut end around the top of the glass. Pull the nylon piece down the outside of the glass until the toe is just touching the bottom on the inside.

4. Pour the grass seeds down the nylon tube in the glass so they end up at the toe.

5. Pour the sawdust on top of the grass seeds. Don't mix the seeds and sawdust together.

6. Very gently, push the cut end of the nylon back to the top of the glass. Pull the nylon tube out of the glass.

7. Starting at the toe, draw up the nylon with your hand so that it is smooth and tight around the seeds and sawdust. Squeeze the nylon together above them.

8. Ask someone to wrap the fishing line just under where you are squeezing and tie a tight knot. Make sure there are no gaps between the nylon and the sawdust and seeds.

✋ **9.** Cut off the extra nylon.

10. Draw eyes, a nose, a mouth, and anything else you like with fabric paint.

11. Sprout the Earth Buddy by following the instructions at the beginning of this book.

Growing Earth Buddy plants is only the beginning. There's a whole world of plants — in sidewalk cracks, in flower boxes, in gardens and fields — just waiting for you to discover and learn more about. Find these plants and watch how they grow. Look after the ones that need your help. And spread the word — plants are amazing!

WORDS THAT WILL GROW ON YOU

Here are some words that you will find in this book, along with other words about plants and growing.

Chlorophyll
A chemical in plants that makes their leaves green. Plants use chlorophyll, along with sunlight, water, and air, to make food for themselves.

Compost
A mixture of plant matter that breaks down, or decomposes, and turns into "soil food" that you can give to other plants. Tiny plants and animals eat the plants and turn them into "soil food" for other plants.

Embryo
A tiny baby plant found inside a seed.

Germination
The process by which seeds start to grow and sprout. Seeds germinate when they have water, warmth, and light.

Photosynthesis
The process by which green plants make their own food. Plants use sunlight, water, and air during photosynthesis.

Root
A root is found at the bottom of the plant. It holds the plant in the ground, sucks up water and nutrients from the soil, and helps send them up the plant to the stems and leaves.

Seed
A baby plant covered by tough skin or shell. A seed also contains food to help the plant grow. It needs sun, water, and warmth to sprout.

Seedling
A young plant that has grown from a seed. A seedling still has some growing to do before it becomes an "adult" plant.

Stem
The "spine" of the plant. A stem holds up the plant to the sun. It carries water to the leaves and also carries food made by the leaves to the rest of the plant.